Harrison Wheelock

Guide and Map of Reese River and Humboldt

Harrison Wheelock

Guide and Map of Reese River and Humboldt

ISBN/EAN: 9783337715236

Printed in Europe, USA, Canada, Australia, Japan

Cover: Foto ©Andreas Hilbeck / pixelio.de

More available books at **www.hansebooks.com**

GUIDE

AND

MAP OF REESE RIVER

AND

HUMBOLDT:

CONTAINING

CORRECT AND VALUABLE INFORMATION OF THE COUNTRY
AND MINES; PROCESS OF TESTING AND ASSAYING
ORES; FORM OF TRUST DEED; CERTIFICATE
OF INCORPORATION; LIGHTNING CAL-
CULATOR; CALENDAR FOR 1864,
AND TABLE OF DISTANCES.

BY

HARRISON WHEELOCK.

SAN FRANCISCO:
TOWNE & BACON, BOOK, JOB, AND CARD PRINTERS,
No. 536 Clay Street, opposite Leidesdorff.
1864.

PREFACE.

This publication, as its name indicates, is intended as a guide to those who may visit that section of country known as the Reese River and Humboldt Mines; and also to impart valuable information to that numerous class of persons who have interests in those newly discovered and wonderfully rich mineral sections.

Whatever merit it may possess consists in the knowledge the writer has acquired of those sections of country from careful personal observations, with the view of presenting the facts so obtained to the public, and the truthful manner in which they are presented. The impossibility of any person being able to give an extensive and minutely correct description of a country embracing so large an area of territory as is included in this publication, of which but little until very recently has been known, will, doubtless, serve as an excuse for any mistakes or inaccuracies that may be discovered.

Believing that the knowledge herein given, to obtain which from personal observation involves no inconsiderable amount of time, expense, and trouble, will be of incalculable benefit to capitalists who wish to invest their means, as well as to the thousands who are rushing to the Reese River and Humboldt Mines, with but a meager knowledge of the country, the writer fully realizes the importance of giving reliable information, therefore facts are stated, regardless of the effect they may have upon individual or incorporated interests.

The accompanying Map will be of great service to all desirous of obtaining a correct idea of the mines. No expense or trouble has been spared to make it what it professes to be, a most reliable and truthful representation of the Reese River and Humboldt Mining Country. The principal towns, mountains, streams, cañons, and mining localities, are given with an accuracy which could only be secured by such untiring energy, patience, and skill as has been exhibited by the compiler and draughtsman, M. Milleson, Esq.

Hoping that the benefits anticipated by the writer may, at least in part, be realized by those under whose observation this publication may come, it is submitted without further comment.   H. W.

San Francisco, 1864.

REESE RIVER MINES.

Routes to the Mines.

So much has been written concerning the routes to the Reese River and Humboldt mines, and the best method of reaching them, within the past year, that it is hardly necessary to express an opinion upon this subject. However, for the benfit of those who may not know how to secure the *few* conveniences and comforts incident upon so tedious a trip the following is offered—for what it is worth. The distance from Sacramento to Austin is three hundred and fifty miles, to accomplish which, by stage, requires about three days and nights, constant travel. The numerous hotels already established on all the stage routes from Sacramento to Virginia and Carson cities, and the conveniences afforded to travelers, renders it quite immaterial which route one selects as regards comforts. So also in regard to the scenery, any person that has never crossed the Sierras will find the magnificence and grandeur of the scenery on either route quite sufficient to make the trip highly interesting and satisfactory. The road from Virginia City to Austin and Humboldt is decidedly a "hard road to travel," much of the way being a loose alkali soil, the least disturbance of which causes a continual dust to rise, which is necessarily inhaled by man and beast greatly to their discomfort. The entire absence of all luxuries, and even conveniences at the public houses on the road, together with the scarcity of good water, and the barrenness of the country makes it anything but a pleasure trip. However, there is much to interest and instruct one of a patient and philosophical turn of mind. Especially will an excellent opportunity be afforded to "let patience have her perfect work."

The stage fare from Sacramento to Virginia City is twenty-five dollars, and from Virginia to Austin about forty dollars, varying according to the competition, thereby costing in the neighborhood of seventy dollars to go from Sacramento to Austin, aside from personal expenses, the amount of which depends upon the economy or extravagance practiced by the individual travelers. A journey in a private conveyance or on horseback from Virginia City to Austin or any other part of the mines is by many considered far preferable. The expense is no more and, although it takes a few hours longer to perform the journey, the unpleasant night travel without sleep and the dust experienced by stage is almost entirely avoided. Horses can be purchased in Virginia or Carson for from forty to seventy-five dollars that will carry a man through to Reese River or Humboldt comfortably in four or five days, and if properly taken care of will be as valuable in the end as at the commencement of the journey. This is by far the cheapest and most pleasant way of reaching the mines, in the estimation of those whose experience enables them to judge correctly. An ordinary suit of clothes and two pairs of blankets will be sufficient to enable a man to make the trip comfortably and furnish lodgings for himself. Some considerable expense may be avoided, also, by taking a supply of edibles, as one dollar is the cost of the most common meal on the road.

The best time to go is in April, or the first of May for those who intend to prospect, as the weather, judging from last year, will be unpleasant, and unfavorable for prospecting purposes up to that time. However, persons wishing to secure claims, and town property, by purchase in the various "cities" in the mining regions, will do well to go much earlier, so as to be ahead of the immense rush that will evidently take place in that direction at an early day.

Towns in Reese River.

The following comprises all the principal towns or cities in the Reese River country, at the present time, without reference to their estimated importance :

AUSTIN AND CLIFTON,

Are the oldest and by far the most populous towns in Reese River, being situated in Reese River District and in the same cañon adjoining each other. They will no doubt, as they already are merging into each other to some extent, become in due time one and the same town and city.

Water is by no means abundant, nor of the best quality ; still, there is a sufficient quantity for all practicable purposes. Lumber is as plentiful, in the vicinity of Austin, as in most other localities, consisting of small pine trees, altogether unsuitable for building purposes, but valuable for timbering tunnels, fencing, and fuel.

JACOBSVILLE,

Is a small town situated on Reese River, seven miles west of Austin. It consists of one hotel, two or three stores, one quartz mill, and quite a number of residences. The soil in the immediate vicinity is not fertile unless an abundant growth of sage brush and grease wood may be considered an indication of that condition. However, the soil is excellent for manufacturing adobes, the superior quality of which for building purposes is evidenced by the fact that some of the finest buildings in Austin are composed of them.

YANKEE BLADE,

Is located four miles north of Austin, in a pleasant ravine, quite accessible from the valley for teams, with sufficient water for one or two quartz mills and other needful purposes, and is surrounded with an abundance of timber such as the Reese River country affords, which makes it much more desirable than many other localities. A considerable number of families have settled in this place. The general appearance of thrift and enterprise exhibited gives evidence of its growth and future importance.

AMADOR, OR CORAL CITY,

Lies four miles north of Yankee Blade, in Amador District, and although one of the youngest, bids fair to out-rival some of the older and more populous towns. Its natural advantages are not superior to those of the towns before-mentioned, and the rich mines that have been discovered in its immediate vicinity are its main attraction.

CASON CITY,

Or Big Creek, as the principal town on that stream is called, is situated twelve miles south of Austin, in the mouth of Big Creek Cañon, and in Big Creek District, possesses all the natural advantages, as likewise do the other towns on Big Creek, requisite for pleasant populous and thriving places. The large and pure stream of water, one of the largest in the Reese River country, alone, to say nothing of the ample supply of timber in the cañon or ravine through which this noble stream courses, is sufficient to attract attention and induce persons to make it their residence. The same may be said of

LANDER CITY,

Situated two miles below Cañon City, on the same stream. The liberality and enterprise of the Shoshone Company, who own a large tract of land including this place, together with the advantages it possesses over many other towns, renders it a desirable residence for families. The soil in the vicinity is exceedingly fertile and productive, with good facilities for irrigation. From experiments already made, it is evident that the soil is capable of producing vegetables and produce of nearly every description, if properly tilled.

A fine quartz mill is being put up at this place by T. G. Phelps & Co., at a cost of $75,000. It is expected to be in running order sometime in April with ten stamps, and arrangements have been made for ten more to be added in a short time. The water power is obtained from Big Creek, which is sufficient to run eighty stamps. The water-wheel is forty feet in diameter, and three feet breast. The commendable energy and perseverance of the gentlemen engaged in this enterprise will not only add much to the importance of Lander City, but also be the means of rapidly developing the mineral resources of Big Creek District. The same may be said in regard to the steam quartz mill at Cañon City, which has been in operation several months, and has done and is still doing satisfactory work. Another water-mill just above, on the same stream, is well under way, while the numerous mill-sites, already located along the entire cañon is evidence of the intentions of other enterprising parties, and of the bright prospects of this section in the future.

WATERTOWN,

Lying between the two cities above named, will eventually, doubtless, become a part of one of the largest and most populous places in the Reese River country, consisting of Lander City, Watertown, Cañon City, Mineral City, adjoining Cañon City above, and Montrose still further up the cañon at the junction of two ravines, through one of which the toll road to the summit leading to Pleasant Valley runs, and the other leading to Geneva and Smoky Valley.

MONTROSE,

On account of its pleasant and valuable locality at the intersection of the two roads before mentioned will, it is claimed by many, of necessity become of more importance than any other point in the cañon. By reference to the map, it will be seen that there is some reason for such a prediction, as it is situated in the

1*

made of some of the most extensive and richest ledges in the District. Besides, its water privileges are inferior to no other place, and the probability is that the overland stage road will run through Big Creek Cañon, thereby shortening the distance of the present route from fifteen to twenty-five miles.

It is but justice to observe, that the enterprising proprietors of this place, Messrs. Broadhead, Barnes & Rogers, are entitled to no little credit for their liberality to residents and strangers, which have given an impetus and importance to the place that it would not otherwise possess. A goodly number of buildings are completed and occupied by families, and many more are being built, which already is an earnest of the grand terminus of the future thriving and populous town to be composed of the several places above named.

GENEVA,

Is situated at the mouth of Birch Creek Cañon, in Big Smoky District, on the eastern side of the range of mountains, some twelve miles from Austin and eight miles from Cañon City. Aside from the rich and extensive ledges in the immediate vicinity, it has nothing particularly attractive as a place of residence, except the fine stream of pure cold water with which it is favored. It contains but one public house and three or four private residences. The illiberality of the proprietors of this place, it is said, has heretofore retarded its growth. Preparations have been made for erecting one or more large quartz mills in the spring, which will no doubt attract a large number of people, and make it a place of considerable importance in a few months' time.

GUADALAJARA,

Is the name of a mining camp at the mouth of a deep cañon on the same side of the mountains as Geneva, in Santa Fe District, sixteen miles south of that place. Although it has been surveyed and blocked off for a town or city, its chances for becoming a place of any considerable importance in the future are limited, in consequence of the superior advantages afforded for a town site at the mouth of Big Smoky Cañon, four miles south of it, in the same district.

This locality is accessible for teams from Austin *via* Smoky Valley, and also will be *via* Big Creek through Pleasant Valley, as soon as the toll road is completed over the summit.

The stream issuing from the mouth of this spacious cañon, called Big Smoky Creek, is supplied from the numerous ravines making into the main cañon on either side for eight or ten miles, furnishing an inexhaustible supply of water for any number of quartz mills.

WASHINGTON,

The principal town in Washington District, is thirty-five miles south-east of Austin, and bids fair to become a place of much importance. It already contains a population of several hundred inhabitants, a majority of whom are Italians, Mexicans, and Austrians. The town has been laid out evidently with the expectation of its becoming a large and populous place, if not a city. A short distance from Washington, is

NEW HOPE,

A settlement, which, if it does not lay claim to the high sounding title of city, has some pretensions as to the future, as its cheerful and hopeful name indicates.

Mining Districts.

The following comprises all the districts in what is called the Reese River or Toyabee Range of Mountains, in regular order, commencing with

MOUNT VERNON DISTRICT,

The most northerly yet formed, embraces Boon's Cañon, some thirty miles north of Austin. Having been recently formed, there has been comparatively but little prospecting done ; but like all other new districts, there are sufficient indications in the ledges prospected to warrant the belief that the district abounds in rich ledges, that only need developing to attract attention. The reports from there are exceedingly encouraging, and being in the same range of mountains with other rich districts, it is but reasonable to conclude that Mount Vernon District will equal if not exceed many older mining localities.

MOUNT HOPE DISTRICT,

Is situated about eighteen miles north of Austin, on the Reese River Valley side of the range; it is tolerably well watered and timbered, and contains many rich and undeveloped ledges. The indications exhibited by the croppings of many of the ledges and the rich assays obtained, give unmistakable evidence of the immense mineral wealth embraced within this district. There is no reason, from present appearances, why this may not become one of the most important districts in the country. The limited amount of prospecting that has been done, compared with many other districts, is the only reason that it does not attract more attention at the present time. If the indications already obtained are reliable, which no one doubts, Mount Hope will yield immense fortunes to the "lucky" miners who develop their ledges during the present season. The most notable ledges already located, consist of Silver King, Indian Guide, Mary Loo, Emerald Isle, Henry Clay, Ladona, Mountain Maid, Pride of the Mountain, Northern Light, Rothschild, Palmetto, Rainbow, Rising Sun, Star of the West, Trieste, Scandinavian, Morning Star, Phillips, Mountain Boy, Empire State, and Lone Star.

The laws of the district are similar to those of the Reese River District, which are given in another place, and only differ from them in some unessential particulars to suit the locality.

AMADOR DISTRICT,

Adjoining Mount Hope on the south, extends from Reese River Valley on the west, to the summit on the east, and runs south to the Reese River District. It embraces the foot-hills between the valley and the mountains, and the most famous ledge within its borders, after which the district is named, is located in one of these foot-hills. The discovery of the Amador ledge last November, which proved to be exceedingly rich and large, created great excitement at the time, and attracted the attention of a large number of miners and speculators, and is by many considered the richest mineral district in Reese River. Whether the numerous ledges located in the vicinity of the Amador are rich, is a question yet to be decided, although the chances of their being so are favorable. Probably there has been more time and capital employed in prospecting in this district than in any other excepting Reese River District, hence its present importance and wide-spread notoriety. There is no reason to suppose that any other district would not become equally famous for its rich and extensive ledges, with the same amount of labor and capital expended.

The following is a list of the names of some of the ledges located, some known to be rich and others supposed to be, in this district: Amador, Coral, Rough and Ready, Gen. Banks, Conqueror, Belmont, Ivanhoe, Old Hickory, Forty-Nine, Union Flag, Legal Tender, Wild Wood, Tunnel, Batavia, Herkimer, Huron, Seneca, John Adams, Quincy, Delhi, Excelsior. A few months' time will determine whether the richness of this district will warrant the great expectations indulged in by the discovery of the rich ledges already made. Upwards of three hundred claims have been recorded.

REESE RIVER DISTRICT,

Is the oldest, and contains the greatest number of rich lodes as well as the greatest number of worthless

ones, of any district in the country : the most of which
are very narrow and not really entitled to the name of
lodes. These numerous rich veins of decomposed quartz
are found in the bed rock and running in every conceiv-
able direction, intersecting each other, thereby caus-
ing great perplexity and dispute between the different
claimants. The reasonable supposition is, that there is
one main lode not yet discovered in which these small
veins terminate. Doubtless, with the hope of striking
this supposed lode, a number of tunnels are being
run at different points. A large number of "blind
ledges" have been discovered, some of which are
very valuable. Various methods have been adopted
to find them. As they do not crop out above the surface, luck is considered a necessary prerequisite for
success in hunting for them. However, there are
various signs, such as the appearance of float rock on
the surface, the shape of the ground, and the color of
the soil, that are considered by experienced prospectors
as sure indications of the existence of a ledge near by.
Where these indications are discovered, holes are dug
and narrow cuts run, resulting in success or failure
according to the good or bad "luck" of the prospectors.
When the surface is sufficiently smooth to allow a fur-
row to be made with a plow, which is the case in many
places, the easiest and most expeditious way of finding
these invisible rich streaks is, to discard the pick and
shovel and resort to the use of a yoke of oxen and plow.
Then if there be any ledges that come up within a few
inches of the surface, they are sure to be discovered,
when an examination can be instituted as to their value
or worthlessness. This novel method of prospecting for
blind ledges has in some instances amply rewarded
prospectors in this famous district.

A large majority of the ledges as yet discovered in
Reese River District are very narrow, although there
are many of good size and immensely rich. The following comprises what are considered some of the most
valuable claims: Oregon, Morgan & Muncey, Union

No. 2, Yankee Blade, Cicero, Black Swan, Ontario,
Black Hawk, Sonora, Tesora, Vineyard, Capital, Oro
Fino, McManus, Sailor, Illinois, Savage, Sampson,
Florida, Pizarro, Mount Providence, Real del Monte,
Lancaster, San Miguel, Lepine, North Star, Troy,
Vesta, Dunkirk, Bamboo, Magnolia, Oak Branch,
Providential, Mills, Post & White, consolidated, Polar
Star, Como Tunnel Co., Rough Crown Diamond, Achilles, Cashel, Fortuna, Star of Nevada, Murphy, Lady of
Lyons, Juno, Honest Miner No. 2, Marshall, Revenue,
Howard, and some two thousand others, many of which
are doubtless as rich as those enumerated. Over
twenty-five hundred claims have been located and recorded in this district.

REESE RIVER CANAL.

This important and expensive enterprise, commenced
in November, 1863, and now about completed by
Messrs. T. F. Gould and H. Farley, cannot fail to be
of great advantage to the mining interests of Reese
River and Amador districts, inasmuch as it brings the
water of Reese River over a mile nearer the mines,
thereby creating a large number of fine mill sites, supplying a thousand inches of water, and sufficient fall to
propel the largest kind of machinery. Neither can the
value of the immense water power furnished by this
canal be too highly estimated, in view of the scarcity
and expense of fuel in the vicinity.

While the enterprising gentlemen above-mentioned
are likely to reap a rich reward for their perseverance
and energy, those interested in the mines will be more
or less benefited by this successful and profitable undertaking.

COLOSSAL LEDGE,

Is the name of a very large ledge running quartering
across the range of mountains in the vicinity of the
town of Yankee Blade, and can be traced some two
miles and a half. It is mentioned only as a noteworthy

fact of the uniting of the two formations, slate and granite, of which it appears to be the dividing line, having a foot-wall of granite and a hanging-wall composed of a mixture of slate and porphery. Whether this is the grand mother ledge as many suppose, on account of its dividing the two formations, and in which all or most of the numerous narrow ledges terminate, time and labor can alone determine.

SIMPSON'S PARK DISTRICT,

Adjoins Reese River District on the south, extends from the valley on the west to the summit of the mountains on the east.

Veatch's Cañon, named after the pioneer of this district, Dr. Veatch, affords accessible egress and ingress from the valley into where the principal ledges are located. A number of valuable claims have long been located, upon which considerable work has been done, with the most favorable prospects. The best judges of silver-bearing rock and experienced miners express the utmost confidence in the claims located in this section. The fact that there are only sixty-two claims recorded in this district, may be considered good evidence that the most of them afford unmistakable indications of richness, which fact is generally acknowledged by all who have had an opportunity of testing them. The granite and slate formation unite in this district and the ledges are larger and better defined generally than in Reese River District. The indisputable evidence of the mineral value of these mines are manifested, in the rock procured from the Lord Byron, Idaho, and Mount Prospect.

BIG CREEK DISTRICT,

Is bounded on the north by Simpson's Park, and on the south by Washington District, a distance of ten or twelve miles. The large ravine or cañon through which Big Creek runs is about in the center of the district, and affords the easiest and most natural and accessible route for travel across the mountains to be found any where in this range, excepting, perhaps, in the vicinity of Austin. Upon the sides of the main cañon, and in the numerous ravines running into it, and also upon the mountains adjacent, many large and well-defined ledges have been discovered, the rock of which assays sufficiently rich to cause those interested to indulge in bright visions of wealth. If the ledges do not equal in richness many of those found in Reese River District, their extensiveness and width, together with the fact that they are well defined, more than makes up for the difference. The slate formation, the appearance of float rock on the surface, the character of the rock, and the general indications in this district are such as to warrant the belief of scientific men, whose opinions are important, but of course not always correct, that this district contains as rich silver bearing rock as can be found in the Reese River country.

The extensive preparations made to prospect these ledges, and the great expense already incurred by different companies, shows a confidence in the richness of these claims on the part of those thus engaged that cannot fail to exert a favorable impression upon the minds of those who design to pitch their prospecting tent in a rich mining locality. The abundance of pure water and fine timber that abounds within its limits, in a country where these indispensable articles are scarce, is another strong inducement for persons to settle in the Big Creek District. The following are some of the claims, upon several of which a large amount of work has been done, with the most flattering prospects :

Great Eastern, Great Western, Florence, Dutch Claim, Dahlgren, Teachers' Ledge, General Meade, Leviathan, Josephine, Sultana, Virginia Lee, Hancock, Ethan Allen, Chatfield, Granite State, Charleston, Fairview, Wheeler & Rogers, Montrose, Mineral Star, Virginia, Astor Ledge, Climate, Constitution, Seely Ledge, Martinique, Monitor, Ratler, Canada, Belle Union, American, Sunlight, Poor Man, Arago, Gold Point, St. Marys.

Besides these, over eight hundred claims have been located in this district, many of which are undoubtedly worthless, by the numerous prospectors that have explored the country, claiming everything that had the appearance of a ledge, regardless of their value or utter worthlessness, vainly hoping that some one of them might prove valuable. Hence, it is necessary to exercise judgment and discrimination in purchasing or locating claims in this district, as well as in others. There are other districts, however, the ledges of which exhibit indications of richness equal to if not in some instances far superior to those in Big Creek District. Among which, is

SMOKY DISTRICT,

Situated on the opposite side of the range of mountains, extending from the summit to Smoky Valley on the east, and to Santa Fe District on the south. Many of the ledges are noted for being of immense size, and containing an inexhaustible amount of minerals of various kinds. A sufficient amount of good water, as well as timber, abounds in this district for all practicable purposes. A number of claims are being prospected, and no inconsiderable amount of capital has been and is still being invested, to develop the numerous ledges.

The following may be considered the leading or representative claims: Smoky Valley Ledge, Everett, Mount Vernon, Mammoth, Gipsey Queen, St. Clair, Olive Branch, Keystone, Alladin, Napoleon, San Francisco. In addition to these, some seven hundred have been located.

SANTA FE DISTRICT,

Adjoining Big Smoky on the south, includes a large extent of territory. consisting of high rugged mountains, well watered, with a meager amount of timber. Its ledges, however, judging from appearances and discoveries already made, are second to no others, and are attracting no little attention from capitalists and prospectors. Like many other districts, it will require much more labor and expense to fully develop its rich mineral wealth, the evidence of the existence of which is an established fact. The claims that have already attracted attention, are the Otho and Extension, King, Boston, Maryland, Mammoth, Imperatrice, San Francisco, Belle, Veatch, Santa Maria, Mother of Ledges, Silver Light, Diadem, Ingot, Rising Sun, Indian Queen, and Loyal Ledge; together with three hundred others, the prospecting of which will in due time reveal their value.

SUMMIT DISTRICT,

Joins Santa Fe on the south, and is second to no other in the abundance of good water and timber with which it is supplied. Pleasant Valley extends from the summit or western extremity of the district to Smoky Valley, a distance of eight or ten miles, and is all that its name indicates. It is one of the most delightful localities in the territory, containing many acres of good soil, watered by the numerous little streams that constitute Big Smoky Creek, and being surrounded by high bluff mountains, it is in a great measure shielded from the severe storms and winds that sometimes prevail.

The mines have caused in times past no little excitement among miners, and the size and number of ledges visible, already located, together with the rich prospects obtained, has induced a number of wealthy capitalists to invest a large amount for the purpose of developing them. The appearance and character of the ledges are similar to those found in adjoining districts. The location of Summit District, its natural advantages, and the immense mineral wealth contained within its borders, of which the best of evidence is afforded, must necessarily in a very short time attract more than usual attention. Between two and three hundred claims have been recorded, a few of which are being energetically prospected, with good signs of ultimate success. The following are worthy of being mentioned: Alhambra, Ledge (consolidated) Gem, Osceola, Phœnix, Chin Ledge, Willow Ledge, Queen Ledge, Vanderbilt, Ingomar, and Nevere. Besides, many others, the rock of which assays equally good.

LA PLATA DISTRICT,

Is situated about forty miles south of Santa Fe, on the same side of the range of mountains. But little is known of the mines within its boundaries, as scarcely any prospecting has been done. There are, however, some good indications of the existence of silver-bearing rock, on the sides of the steep, barren, rugged mountains, and in the deep, narrow cañons, for which this section is noted. Two large fine streams are found in this district, while timber is very scarce.

SMOKY CHIMNEY DISTRICT,

Lies between Santa Fe and La Plata, attracting but little attention, although numerous claims have been located by the early and eager prospectors, who have immortalized themselves by posting notices wherever they went, regardless of the waste of paper.

WASHINGTON DISTRICT,

Is situated on the Reese River Valley side of the mountains, and is bounded on the north by Big Creek District, and on the south by Marysville District. A large number of claims have been located, and a very considerable amount of prospecting has been done.

The specimens of rich rock that have been procured by prospectors, together with some very valuable claims that have been discovered, has given Washington District an enviable reputation, which has resulted favorably for that locality. Water and timber are as plentiful as in most other districts. Some of the most noted claims are the New Hope, Sacramento, Geneva, Mobile, Live Oak, St. Louis, Columbia, Trinidad, Revenue, San Fernando, San Domingo No. 2, Stranger, Don Quixote,

Santa Rosa, and Mattie Ann. The Reese River Enterprise Co. also indulges in " great expectations." Over
eleven hundred claims have been recorded, and yet there
is room for more.

MARYSVILLE DISTRICT

Joins Washington on the south, embracing a section
very similar in appearance, and containing many quartz
ledges, the testing of which has proven that the discovery of valuable mines only depends upon the development of the ledges located and those to be discovered.
These comprise the principal districts formed at present
in the Toyabee, or Reese River range of mountains.
There are others, however, outside of this range, which
are included in what is called the Reese River Mines ;
and some of which have attracted as much attention, in
consequence of the discovery of rich minerals within
their borders, as many of those before mentioned.

SAN ANTONIO DISTRICT,

Situated about one hundred miles nearly south of
Austin, in a range of mountains on the eastern side of
Smoky Valley, has the reputation of containing some
fabulously rich silver bearing rock. The large number
of prospectors that have visited this district, and the
favorable reports brought back, is pretty good evidence
of the existence of silver and other minerals in this
far-off locality. The greatest obstacle in the way of
speedily developing the mines in this district, is the
scarcity of timber and water. The ledges are very
wide, and said to be extremely rich. More than two
hundred claims have been located, among which the
following are considered a fair sample : Savage, Liber-
ty, Refugio, Merrimac, Valenciana, Michigan, Silver
Circle, Buena Espranza, Lander County, Overland,
and Cincinnati. Some of the above named ledges, it is
claimed, are thirty feet wide ; and none of them less
than fifteen, with a very equal distribution of minerals
through the rock.

CORTEZ DISTRICT

Is a little north of San Antonio, and about seventy miles from Austin. Wonderful reports of the discovery of rich mines have also been brought from this district. Nearly three hundred claims have been located, and comparatively but little has been done towards developing them. The Wenban, Mountain Brow, and Farrell, are believed to be rich.

UNION DISTRICT

Is in the Shoshone range of mountains, some sixty miles south-west of Austin. Some very rich specimens of silver ore have been found. The indications generally are very favorable and encouraging, and consequently over five hundred claims have been located already.

RAVENSWOOD DISTRICT

Lies on the western side of Reese River Valley, nearly opposite Amador District, and some eighteen miles from Austin. There has never been any great excitement created by the discoveries made, although it is well known to contain some rich and valuable ledges. About one hundred claims are taken up in this district.

AUGUSTA DISTRICT

Is near the Overland Stage Road, thirty-five miles west of Austin. An abundance of timber and water is found, and the ledges are large and well defined, but not claimed to be extremely rich, although sufficiently so to warrant prospecting and labor upon them. Over two hundred claims have been recorded.

General Remarks.

Although the description given of the Reese River mines may appear to be highly colored, in consequence of the statement that every district yet formed contains a greater or lesser number of ledges of rich silver bearing rock, nevertheless it is an indisputable fact, which is fully established by the evidences obtained from personal observation and other reliable sources. Over six thousand claims have been located already in the various districts enumerated, and probably nearly that number in the Humboldt mines; and although it be true that a large proportion of these claims are worthless, yet that there are a sufficient number of rich ones distributed throughout this vast extent of territory to make it the richest mineral country ever discovered, no one at all acquainted with the country and the character of the mines can deny.

A particular account of the many valuable mines discovered in different sections of the country, the value of which is universally acknowledged, has necessarily been omitted, on account of the impossibility of doing them justice in a work of this size, and at the same time to avoid making an invidious distinction between them. The inexhaustible mineral resources of these sections of country are apparent to every one, however uninviting may be their barren mountains and arid deserts. The knowledge of the existence of the precious metals in such great abundance in these new and distant regions is of course the cause of the great rush thither, as was the case with California when gold was first discovered. The deprivations and sufferings incident to the settlement of all new countries occasion the expression of opinions at first unfavorable to the climate, soil, etc., invariably—not even excepting those countries noted for the salubrity of their climate and the fertility of their soil. Hence the dismal reports circulated by those who may not have been successful in the Reese River and Humboldt countries should be received with caution, as time and experience may prove these first impressions to be erroneous, as has been the case with California; and there is no reason why these portions of Nevada Territory may not at no distant day become as noted for their agricultural resources as that State.

Although there are numerous waste places, alkali

plains, barren mountains, and "worlds" of sage brush and grease wood, yet from experiments made during the past year it is evident that the soil is sufficiently productive, if properly tilled, to supply nearly all kinds of produce that may be required by the rapidly-increasing population. A very considerable portion of the country is excellent for grazing, particularly on the western side of the Toyabee mountains, including the numerous foot hills, ravines, and portions of Reese River Valley, that produce a luxuriant growth of bunch grass, upon which cattle thrive finely. The valley is quite productive in "spots," and is already dotted over with ranches that bid fair to amply remunerate the owners. The high price of good land in the vicinity of Austin, Big Creek, and other localities, shows the great value attached to it by those whose experience and long residence in the country enable them to judge correctly.

The climate is similar to that of the mining regions of California; and but for the scarcity of timber and water in many places, would compare favorably with the mining districts of that State.

The sickness that has prevailed to some considerable extent may be attributed more to privations, the use of unwholesome water, and exposure in going to the Reese River country, than to any deleterious influence indiginous to the climate. The establishing of hotels on the routes, and the provisions being made for the comfort of travelers, will continually lessen these difficulties, and in a very short time render a journey to that part of the territory a pleasure trip, instead of what it has been, an unpleasant undertaking. Without claiming the gift of prophesy, it may be safely predicted, from the rapid improvement made during the past few months, that within a few years, at most, a railroad will connect this rich and extensive mineral country with the principal cities and towns of California. The imperative demand for such a road, and the favorable condition of the surface of the country over which it will pass, to say nothing of the immense income it will furnish the projectors and the incalculable benefit it will be to the inhabitants, as a means of travel and transportation, cannot fail to inaugurate and rapidly complete this important enterprise.

Thus much is said not for the purpose of extolling the country or its mines beyond what the facts will warrant, nor for the benefit of any individual interest, but merely to convey a truthful representation of the present condition of the country, and its probable future, providing the future may be judged by the past.

It is well known that the country never can afford some of the conveniences and many of the luxuries enjoyed in other localities, owing to its peculiar state and condition ; still it cannot be denied that time and labor will do much towards supplying it with all that is necessary for the prosperity and advancement of an enterprising population. The scarcity of water in some localities can in time be easily overcome by obtaining it from the numerous springs and ever-living streams of pure water that course through the mountain gorges, by means of tunneling, ditching, or fluming, so that this most serious objection can be obviated to a great extent. And so of timber : there is, undoubtedly, a sufficient quantity to meet the demand, excepting for building purposes, until means can be supplied to furnish it at living prices.

A rich and extensive field has been opened up to the industrious, energetic, and enterprising, by the discovery of minerals in Reese River and Humboldt, the result of which can only be anticipated. Without claiming for these particular localities superiority over others equally rich, perhaps, it is evident that they afford an opportunity for as safe and profitable investment as any other. The amount of minerals contained in the successive range of mountains, embracing thousands of miles of territory, precludes the possibility of its ever being exhausted, while the labor and expense employed in developing the mines will only increase their value.

The present moral condition of the people is any

thing but inviting to the pious and devout, although there is not probably any more crime committed or dishonesty practised than in all new mining countries. The wild excitement that prevails, the eagerness with which every one is striving to obtain wealth, and the absence of moral restraint, tends to produce an indifference, and, in many cases, utter disregard of moral principles and rectitude, which results in crime, excess, and evil indulgences, to an alarming extent. However, this condition of things will gradually change for the better, as the population increases and the influence of civilization advances. Already a commendable interest is being exhibited by the residents, in the more populous localities, for the establishment of schools and churches, which augurs well for the future, as is proven by the report of M. J. Ryan, School Census Marshal of Lander County. In fact, the country furnishes ample material for the highest state of physical and moral development. The means for the transmission of news, by express and telegraph, are being rapidly extended, and will in a very short period connect the most distant localities with the most important and populous places, Big Creek and Austin.

Mining Laws of Reese River District.

The following laws of Reese River District, are similar in most respects to those adopted for all the other mining districts. In some, more or less labor is required on claims to secure them against being jumped, and also the number of feet allowed each locator or discoverer is varied, according to the views of the residents or miners in the different localities. However, the laws of Reese River District are applicable to any of the other districts, with the above exceptions, and may serve as a guide to those who may not be acquainted with the general mining laws of the Reese River Mines.

SECTION 1. This district shall be known as the Reese River Mining District, and shall be bounded as follows, to wit: On the north by a distance of ten miles from the Overland Telegraph Line, on the east by Dry Creek, on the south by a distance of ten miles from the Overland Telegraph Line, and on the west by Edwards' Creek, where not conflicting with any new districts formed to date.

Sec. 2. There shall be a Mining Recorder elected on the first day of June next for this district, who shall hold office for one year from the seventeenth of June next, unless sooner removed by a new election, which can only be done by a written call, signed by at least fifty claim-holders, giving notice of a new election to be held after said notice shall have been posted and published for at least twenty days in some newspaper published in or nearest this district; and the Recorder shall be a resident of the district.

Sec. 3. It shall be the duty of the Recorder to keep in a suitable book or books a full and truthful record of the proceedings of all public meetings; to place on record all claims brought to him for that purpose, when such claim shall not interfere with or affect the rights and interests of prior locators, recording the same in the order of their date, for which service he shall receive fifty cents for each claim recorded. It shall also be the duty of the Recorder to keep his books open at all times to the inspection of the public; he shall have the power to appoint a deputy to act in his stead, for whose official acts he shall be held responsible. It shall also be the duty of the Recorder to deliver to his successor in office all books, records, papers, etc., belonging to or pertaining to his office.

Sec. 4. All examinations of the record must be made in the full presence of the Recorder or his deputy.

Sec. 5. Notice of a claim or location of mining ground by any individual, or by a company, on file in a Recorder's office, shall be deemed equivalent to a record of the same.

Sec. 6. Each claimant shall be entitled to hold by location two hundred feet on any lead in the district, with all the dips, spurs, and angles, offshoots, outcrops, depths, widths, variations, and all the mineral and other valuables therein contained—the discoverer of and locator of a new lead being entitled to one claim extra for discovery.

Sec. 7. The locator of any lead, lode, or ledge in the district shall be entitled to hold on each side of the lead, lode, or ledge located by him or them, one hundred feet; but this shall not be construed to mean any distinct or parallel ledge within the two hundred feet other than the one originally located.

Sec. 8. All locations shall be made by a written notice posted upon the ground, and boundaries defined, and all claimants' names posted on the notice.

Sec. 9. Work done on any tunnel, cut, shaft, or drift, in good faith, shall be considered as being done upon the claim owned by such person or company.

Sec. 10. Every claim (whether by individual or by company) located, shall be recorded within ten days after the date of location.

Sec. 11. There shall be done for each and every claim of two hundred feet held by any person, persons, or company, one day's work for each and every month, which shall hold said claims for thirty days thereafter; but nothing in this section shall be construed so as to prevent said person, persons, or company from doing the requisite amount of work at any one time, to hold their claims for three months.

Sec. 12. Whenever $1,000 has been expended on the claims of a company in this district, the ground so claimed by the company shall be deemed as belonging in fee to the locators thereof, and their assigns, and the same shall not be subject to location or relocation by other parties forever after, except by an acknowledged abandonment by the company of the ground, which shall be construed to mean an entire abandonment after laying idle for one year, except in cases where claims are in litigation.

Sec. 13. The Recorder shall go upon the ground with any and all parties desiring to locate claims, and shall be entitled to receive for such service, say for a company location, of six or more names, three dollars, and for each location numbering less than six names, fifty cents each. And it shall be his further duty to measure any claim or claims, and make or cause to be made good and sufficient landmarks defining said claim or claims; and he is prohibited from making any location for any person, persons, or company, without complying with this section, and seeing their boundaries fully defined.

Sec. 14. These Rules or Mining Laws may be altered or amended by a two-thirds vote of those present at any meeting in the district, at any time after twenty days' notice of such intention shall have been given in the manner prescribed above, for calling a new election for Recorder.

HUMBOLDT MINES.

THE minuteness with which the Humboldt mines are represented in the accompanying Map, renders it quite unnecessary to give a description of them in this place; but for the purpose of giving a more general idea of the country and the mines, the following is presented upon the authority of Prof. E. A. Scott, who has spent some three years in that region:

The climate is healthy and generally agreeable, while the soil in many places, embracing thousands of acres, is exceedingly fertile, producing, when properly cultivated, all kinds of vegetables and cereals in great abundance. Like the Reese River country, it is superior for grazing purposes. Cattle thrive admirably at all seasons of the year on the fine quality of grass that covers the numerous valleys and hill-sides. Land of a superior quality is found in Paradise, and other large valleys, as well as in many places on the banks of the Humboldt River. Timber is scarce but sufficient for all needful purposes. The water is plentiful and generally good excepting during the dryest seasons, when it is slightly tinctured with a mineral taste, but not sufficient to create sickness or render it particularly unpleasant.

Considerable interest is manifested in the cause of education, and a number of schools have been established and are in a flourishing condition.

The Pi-Ute, Shoshone, and Bannock tribes of Indians are numerous, but perfectly docile and harmless.

The surface of the country is made up of successive chains of mountain ranges and valleys, from ten to fifteen miles across, running in every direction, over, around, or through which good roads exist, so that almost any part of the country is easily accessible.

Many very valuable discoveries of rich silver and gold bearing rock have been made in various districts. The ledges are generally large and well defined. The similar appearance of the rock in many of the newly discovered districts to that found in the older ones, leads to the reasonable supposition that there is an immense amount of minerals in all parts of the country, to obtain which only requires time and labor.

Some of the oldest and most noted districts are located in Star Mountain, and comprise Humboldt, Star, Buena Vista, El Dorado, Echo, Prince Royal, Santa Clara, Indian, American, and Sacramento Districts. The following ledges in the same mountain are known to be valuable: Sheba, Mammoth Series, Mountain Top Series, San Barnard, Washington, Winnemucca, Cuba and Yankee Ledges, together with the Oro Fino, Clear Creek, Neptune, Auld Lang Syne, Crœsus, Eclipse, and many others, in the first east range.

Harmony District has likewise attracted no little attention. It is located in the northern portion of San Francisco Mountain, which lies about forty-five miles from Unionville, in a north-easterly direction from that place. This District was organized in June 1863, by M. Milleson, who located within its boundaries the Grand Central Series of seven ledges, the Gager Series of three ledges, and the Franconi lode, which is a well-defined ledge of 125 feet wide, full of mineral combining Silver, Copper, and Iron. Work to a considerable extent has been done on the above-named ledges both by the original locators and by other parties who have secured extension claims upon them. This District furnishes abundant water-power for mill purposes, and sufficient timber to supply a large population with fuel and for mechanical purposes for a number of years.

The ledges in this District are well defined, of great

width, and bearing ore of the same character of that from the Reese River Districts and of the Dais Padre Mine in Sonora, Mexico.

The Scott and Perigord Tunnel is worthy of note as being one of the grandest enterprises in the country. It was located in 1863, during which time considerable work has been done on it. The eastern mouth of the tunnel is three-fourths of a mile from Star City and in sight of the far-famed Sheba Mine, running through a mountain in the Star Range, a distance of two miles five hundred and twenty-six feet, striking in its passage forty-nine ledges, the most of which exhibit the existence of gold and silver in the rock at or near the surface. Provision has been made by the Company to interest eastern capitalists in this great work, and already means have been taken to push the work with the greatest energy.

Much more might justly be said of different portions of the country, its prospects and resources. However, as the above is only intended to call attention to that section generally, a further description is unnecessary. In justice to the numerous claims in various portions of the territory represented by the map, it will be understood that the mines or ledges particularly noticed thereon, are not claimed to be superior to many others not noticed. It is claimed that the Eureka District is located on the western slope of the Santa Rosa Mountain, and the Santa Rosa District on the Eastern side of the same mountain. However this may be, the valuable mines found in these two districts will soon attract sufficient attention to settle the question of their locality beyond a doubt.

APPENDIX.

METALLURGICAL TESTS.

BY PROF. THOMAS RICE,

Late Lecturer on Chemistry and Metallurgy, Normal Col., Swansea, Wales.

TESTS FOR THE PRESENCE OF COPPER IN ORES.

Pulverize the mineral very fine in a steel or iron mortar; pass the whole through a sieve of 80 holes to the inch, mix your ore thoroughly; take about half a tablespoonful of the fine ore and digest it thoroughly with about half an ounce of nitric acid in a glass vessel (glass flask or beaker); heat the mixture for some time; add to it about two ounces of water; allow the whole to stand at rest until it has subsided; decant or pour off gently the clear liquid, and divide into two parts.

No. 1.—Add a solution of ammonia until the liquid smells strongly of it. If copper be present, a deep azure-blue colored solution will be produced in a few moments.

No. 2.—Immerse in the solution a bright piece of iron, or the blade of a knife. If copper be present, a thin red coating of that metal will be precipitated on the surface of the bright iron.

METHODS FOR DETERMINING THE QUANTITY OF COPPER IN ORES.

Weigh out 50 grains of the pulverized ore, and digest it with a mixture of nitric and sulphuric acids, in equal quantities, in a porcelain crucible capable of holding about three ounces; to the ore add about two ounces of the mixed acid; heat very slowly at first, and cover with a watch-glass; evaporate to dryness; allow the mass to cool; when sufficiently cold to be handled, add to it about two ounces of water; allow it to soak fifteen or twenty minutes; then heat slowly; filter; and to the clear solution add a few drops of hydrochloric acid. Should a white precipitate be produced, filter; and in the solution immerse a piece of bright iron one inch square; heat your solution very slowly, and in about thirty minutes the whole of your copper will be precipitated in the metallic state, on your iron. Clean your copper from the iron; allow the copper precipitate to settle at the bottom of your glass; then pour off your water solution, and to your copper add two or three ounces of hot water, and pour off again when all the copper is collected in the bottom of your vessel; continue doing this until the water is perfectly tasteless. Dry your copper now by placing the vessel containing it over steam; when dry, weigh it; the weight multiplied by two will give you the per centage of copper.

LEAD ORES.

Pulverize the ores as described under the copper tests, and digest a few grains of the ore with nitric acid; add a few ounces of water, and allow the whole to settle; decant your clear solution, and divide into two portions.

No. 1.—Add a solution of common salt in water; a white precipitate dissolved in hot water indicates the presence of lead.

No. 2.—Add a solution of sulphuric acid; a white precipitate will also indicate the presence of lead. Take some of the powdered ore, and mix it with twice its bulk of carbonate of soda; place it in a cavity in a piece of charcoal, and direct a flame on it by means of a blow-pipe; about ten minutes' blowing will produce a button of metallic lead—if it be present in the ore.

QUANTITATIVE ESTIMATION OF LEAD IN ORES.

Weigh out four hundred grains of the ore, and mix it well with the same quantity of carbonate of soda and borax, and transfer it to a red-hot iron crucible in the fire —common fire placed in a blacksmith's forge will do. When the whole is thoroughly melted, increase the heat for a few minutes, and pour the contents of the crucible into an iron mold ; when cold, break up the clay and you will obtain a button of lead, the weight of which divided by four will give you the per centage of lead in the ore. To ascertain the quantity of silver in this, all that is necessary is to heat it in a cupel, (a small dish made of the ashes of bones,) with a good supply of air —a small muffle furnace.

SILVER ORE.

Digest a portion of pulverized ore prepared, as has been described under the head of copper ores, in about one-half ounce pure nitric acid ; when all action has ceased, dilute the solution with about one ounce of distilled water ; filter the solution, and divide into two parts. To No. 1 add a few drops of hydrochloric acid. A precipitate not dissolving in boiling water, but soluble on adding a solution of ammonia, would indicate the presence of silver. No. 2.—Add hydrochloric acid ; collect the precipitate so produced in a small filter ; dry it well and mix it with about twice its bulk of dried carbonate of soda placed in a small cavity in a piece of charcoal, and direct a hot blaze upon it by means of a blow-pipe ; in a few minutes you reduce the silver, and obtain a small metallic button of that metal.

QUANTITATIVE ESTIMATION OF SILVER IN ORES.

Take about 100 grains of the pulverized ore, and mix it with 400 of granulated lead and about 50 grains of fused borax ; place the whole in a dish and heat in a muffle furnace until the whole is thoroughly melted ; keep it in a melted condition and at a bright red heat for about twenty or thirty minutes ; pour the whole contents of the dish into an iron mold, and all the silver and gold will be found alloyed with the lead; place the lead button in a cupel, as described under the head of lead assay; keep your muffle at a good red heat; the lead will be absorbed by the cupel, and a small button of silver will remain on it; just before all the lead is worked away from the silver, you will observe the button rotating very rapidly and emitting an intense light, and all at once become still. When these conditions are completed, all the lead has been driven.

Remove from the furnace, and allow to cool; weigh your button; the weight in 100 grains will be the per centage of silver in the rock; and by proportion you can find out the amount of ounces to the ton; multiply the number of ounces by $1 30, and you will have the value per ton in dollars.

Should this ore contain any gold it will be found alloyed with the silver. Gold is separated from silver by digesting the alloy with pure nitric acid; when all the silver is dissolved, the gold remains, being insoluble; it can then be weighed, and its weight subtracted from that of the alloy, the number of ounces to the ton multiplied 20·69, will give you the value in dollars. If the gold should form a higher proportion than as one is to two of silver, the silver cannot be separated by boiling with nitric acid. In this case, after weighing the button of alloy, sufficient silver must be added to form a suitable alloy for dissolving, and then proceed as above.

Incorporating Claims.

The first thing necessary to be done for incorporating a mining claim is to prepare a Trust Deed; have it signed by the locators of the claim; witnessed before a Notary Public; stamped, and recorded where the claim is located. Then a Certificate of Incorporation must be drawn and signed by at least three Trustees; witnessed before a Notary Public; stamped, and filed in the County Clerk's Office in the County where the claim is located; a certified copy of the same obtained from the County Clerk, and sent to the Secretary of State or Territory, for which a receipt will be given. Then all that is necessary is to procure books and isssue stock. The cost of incorporating a claim, aside from the books and stock, does not exceed $20, unless there be more than an ordinary number of signers of the Trust Deed, providing no expense for executing the necessary papers for incorporation is incurred, the forms of which are here given.

Trust Deed.

This Indenture, made the —— day of —— in the year of our Lord eighteen hundred and sixty —— between the undersigned of the first part, and the —— of the second part, witnesseth, that whereas, the —— has been duly incorporated under the laws of the —— to which it is intended by this instrument to transfer all the right, title, and interest of the parties of the first part which they and each of them have and claim in and to the mining ground and claim or lode and its appurtenances hereinafter described.

Now, therefore, know all men by these presents, that the parties of the first part and each of them whose names are hereunto subscribed, in consideration of Certificates of Stock in said Incorporated Company hereafter to be issued to them, their and each of their heirs and assigns, in conformity with the By-Laws of said Corporation heretofore adopted, do hereby grant, bargain, sell, transfer, remise, release, and quitclaim unto the said ——— its successors and assigns, all their and each of their right, title, interest, claim, and demand whatsoever in law or equity, of, in, or to all that certain mining ground or quartz lode situate, lying, and being on ——— together with all the dips, angles, spurs, and variations of said mining ground and quartz lode, and all and singular the hereditaments and appurtenances thereunto belonging ——— to have and to hold the said premises with their appurtenances unto the said ——— its successors and assigns forever.

In witness whereof said part — of the first part, ha — hereunto set — hand and seal the day and year first above written.

Sealed and delivered in the presence of

Certificate of Incorporation.

——— ss. County of ——— The undersigned having this day formed a corporation for the purpose of mining, do hereby certify that the name of said corporation shall be ———. That the object of said corporation is to carry on and conduct the business of mining on — certain vein or lode known by the name of ——— and situated and recorded in the district of——— known as ———. The amount of the capital stock of said Corporation shall be ——— dollars, which shall be divided into ——— shares, ——— dollars each. The said corporation shall exist for the term of ——— years, and its concerns shall be managed by a Board composed of ——— trustees. The principal place of business of said corporation shall be in the County of ——— where an office shall be kept for the purpose. The following persons, to wit: ———, a majority of whom are citizens of the United States, shall be the trustees to manage the concerns of said corporation for the first three months.

In witness whereof, we have hereunto set our hands and seals ——— this ——— day of A.D. 186 ———.

In presence of ⎱   ——— ——— [L.S.]
               ⎰   ——— ——— [L.S.]
                          ——— ——— [L.S.]

Table of Distances.

			MILES.
Star	City	to Clear Creek District	18
..	..	Oro Fino District	15
..	..	Cinnabar District	35
..	..	Shoshone District	40
..	..	El Dorado	5
..	..	Echo	10
..	..	Sacramento District	20
..	..	American District,	20
..	..	Indian District	22
..	..	St. Mary's District	3
..	..	Trinity District	30
..	..	Antelope District	28
..	..	Silver Mountain District	60
..	..	Central District	20
..	..	Desert District	80
..	..	Augusta District	50
..	..	Eureka	85
..	..	Santa Rosa	75
..	..	Puebla District	150
..	..	Vicksburg District	135
..	..	Monroe's District	160

Lightning Calculator,

Showing the Comparative Value of Gold and Legal Tender Notes (Greenbacks) in the Pacific States, with relation to the Quotations of Gold when commanding a Premium in the great Commercial Cities of the Atlantic Seaboard.

The Currency Basis in the Eastern States is the National Paper Emissions. On the Pacific Coast, Gold is the universally recognized medium of Exchange : consequently, although the quoted premiums on Gold exist, in reality, here as well as East, still, Gold being the basis of businss transactions, the National Currency is not circulated, but is held at a discount, or sold and exchanged (through courtesy) at a certain stated rate per dollar, as if it was an article of merchandise. An erroneous impression has prevailed, that when Gold is held in New York at any certain premium, Legal Tender Notes are of correspondingly less value ; for instance, when Gold is 25 per cent. premium, the opinion exists that the Notes are at a discount of 5 per cent.— whereas (as shown by the Table), the Paper Money is worth 80 cents on the dollar, or at a discount of only 20 per cent.

To facilitate the computation of the assumed relative exchangeable value of these Legal Tender Notes, we have calculated the following tables :

TABLE No. 1.

When gold is at a premium of	The disc'nt on Legal Tender notes is	The net m'ket val. of Legal Tenders is
1 pr.c	$0·0099	$0·9901
2	·0196	·9804
3	·0291	·9709
4	·0385	·9615
5	·0476	·9524
6	·0566	·9434
7	·0654	·9346
8	·0741	·9259
9	·0826	·9174
10	·0909	·9091
11	·0991	·9009
12	·1071	·8929
13	·1150	·8850
14	·1228	·8772
15	·1304	·8696
16	·1379	·8621
17	·1453	·8547
18	·1525	·8475
19	·1597	·8403
20 pr.c	$0·1667	$0·8333
21	·1736	·8264
22	·1803	·8197
23	·1870	·8130
24	·1935	·8065
25	·2000	·8000
26	·2063	·7937
27	·2126	·7874
28	·2188	·7812
29	·2248	·7752
30	·2308	·7692
31	·2366	·7634
32	·2424	·7576
33	·2481	·7519
34	·2537	·7463
35	·2593	·7407
36	·2647	·7353
37	·2701	·7299
38	·2754	·7246
39 pr.c	$0·2806	$0·7194
40	·2857	·7143
41	·2908	·7092
42	·2958	·7042
43	·3007	·6993
44	·3056	·6944
45	·3103	·6897
46	·3151	·6849
47	·3197	·6803
48	·3243	·6757
49	·3289	·6711
50	·3333	·6667
51	·3377	·6623
52	·3421	·6579
53	·3464	·6536
54	·3506	·6494
55	·3548	·6452
56	·3590	·6410
57	·3631	·6369
58 pr.c	$0·3671	$0·6329
59	·3711	·6289
60	·3750	·6250
61	·3789	·6211
62	·3827	·6173
63	·3865	·6135
64	·3902	·6098
65	·3939	·6061
66	·3976	·6024
67	·4012	·5988
68	·4048	·5952
69	·4083	·5917
70	·4118	·5882
71	·4152	·5848
72	·4186	·5814
73	·4220	·5780
74	·4253	·5747
75	·4286	·5714

TABLE No. 2.

This Table is computed to show what amount of Legal Tender Notes can be purchased with any given amount of Gold, when the notes are held at from 40 to 99 cents ($1 being the basis of the calculation).

E. When the price asked for Leg. T. notes is—	F. One dollar in gold will buy in Legal Tender notes—	E. When the price asked for Leg. T. notes is—	F. One dollar in gold will buy in Legal Tender notes—	E. When the price ask'd for Leg. T. notes is—	F. One dollar in gold will buy in Legal Tender notes—	E. When the price ask'd for Leg. T. notes is—	F. One dollar in gold will buy in Legal Tender notes—
$0 40	$2·500000	$0 55	$1·818182	$0 70	$1·428571	$0 85	$1·176471
41	2·439024	56	1·785714	71	1·408451	86	1·162791
42	2·380952	57	1·750877	72	1·388889	87	1·149425
43	2·325581	58	1·724138	73	1·369863	88	1·136364
44	2·272727	59	1·694915	74	1·351351	89	1·123596
45	2·222222	60	1·666667	75	1·333333	90	1·111111
46	2·173913	61	1·639344	76	1·315789	91	1·098901
47	2·127660	62	1·612903	77	1·298701	92	1·086957
48	2·083333	63	1·587302	78	1·282051	93	1·075269
49	2·040816	64	1·562500	79	1·265823	94	1·063829
50	2·000000	65	1·538462	80	1·250000	95	1·052632
51	1·960784	66	1·515152	81	1·234568	96	1·041667
52	1·923077	67	1·492537	82	1·219512	97	1·030928
53	1·886792	68	1·470588	83	1·204817	98	1·020408
54	1·851852	69	1·449275	84	1·190476	99	1·010101

RULE.—Multiply the figures in column marked F (opposite the price asked for the Legal Tender Notes in column E) by the amount of the Gold to be invested, the result will be the amount of notes purchasable therewith.

These calculations being carried to six places of decimals, the variation for any am't not exceeding 1,000,000 will not be appreciable.

RULE.—To find how much Gold would be required to purchase any given amount of Legal Tender Notes, multiply the amount of the notes desired by the rate at which they can be procured, the answer will be the sum of Gold required to purchase the same.

TABLE No. 3.

Gold at premium of—	Disc'nt on Leg.Ten. notes.	Value of Leg.Ten. notes.	Gold at premium of—	Disc'nt on Leg.Ten. notes.	Value of Leg.Ten. notes.
100 pr. c.	·5000	·5000	800 pr.c.	·8889	·1111
200 ··	·6667	·33⅓	900 ··	·9000	·1000
300 ··	·7500	·2500	1,000 ··	·9091	·0909
400 ··	·8000	·2000	2,000 ··	·9524	·0476
500 ··	·8333	·16¾	5,000 ··	·9804	·0196
600 ··	·8571	·1429	9,900 ··	·9900	·0100
700 ··	·8750	·1250			

By this Table it is shown that if Gold should have reached 100 per cent. premium, the Legal Tender Notes would have been valued at 50 cents, and would not have been valueless, as supposed by many. At 400 per cent. premium, the Note is worth 20 cents; at 900 per cent. 10 cents; and at the imaginative value of 9900 per cent., it is still worth 1 cent. Mathematically considered, the Legal Tender Notes can never be valueless.

Thus it appears that the so-called premium on Gold existing throughout the Eastern Money Market, is not so serious an evil as has been generally supposed; and that we have already suffered from as great a depression in the circulating value of the Government issues, as will, in all probability, ever occur again.

Indorsement.

We, the undersigned, having carefully examined the Guide and Map of Reese River and Humboldt, published by H. Wheelock, cheerfully recommend it as being correct in every essential particular.

Hon. T. G. PHELPS,
Capt. M. R. ROBERTS,
Cor. Washington and Stockton Sts., S. F.,
M. H. FARLEY,
305 Montgomery St.,
Prof. E. A. SCOTT,
Agent for the Scott Mining Exploring Co., and Supt. of Public Instruction of Humboldt Co., N. T.

CALENDAR FOR 1864.

	Sund.	Mond.	Tuesd.	Wedn.	Thurs.	Friday	Satur.		Sund.	Mond.	Tuesd.	Wedn.	Thurs.	Friday	Satur.
JAN.						1	2	JULY.						1	2
	3	4	5	6	7	8	9		3	4	5	6	7	8	9
	10	11	12	13	14	15	16		10	11	12	13	14	15	16
	17	18	19	20	21	22	23		17	18	19	20	21	22	23
	24	25	26	27	28	29	30		24	25	26	27	28	29	30
	31								31						
FEB.		1	2	3	4	5	6	AUG.		1	2	3	4	5	6
	7	8	9	10	11	12	13		7	8	9	10	11	12	13
	14	15	16	17	18	19	20		14	15	16	17	18	19	20
	21	22	23	24	25	26	27		21	22	23	24	25	26	27
	28	29							28	29	30	31			
MAR.			1	2	3	4	5	SEPT.					1	2	3
	6	7	8	9	10	11	12		4	5	6	7	8	9	10
	13	14	15	16	17	18	19		11	12	13	14	15	16	17
	20	21	22	23	24	25	26		18	19	20	21	22	23	24
	27	28	29	30	31				25	26	27	28	29	30	
APR.						1	2	OCT.							1
	3	4	5	6	7	8	9		2	3	4	5	6	7	8
	10	11	12	13	14	15	16		9	10	11	12	13	14	15
	17	18	19	20	21	22	23		16	17	18	19	20	21	22
	24	25	26	27	28	29	30		23	24	25	26	27	28	29
MAY.								NOV.	30	31					
	1	2	3	4	5	6	7				1	2	3	4	5
	8	9	10	11	12	13	14		6	7	8	9	10	11	12
	15	16	17	18	19	20	21		13	14	15	16	17	18	19
	22	23	24	25	26	27	28		20	21	22	23	24	25	26
	29	30	31						27	28	29	30			
JUNE.				1	2	3	4	DEC.					1	2	3
	5	6	7	8	9	10	11		4	5	6	7	8	9	10
	12	13	14	15	16	17	18		11	12	13	14	15	16	17
	19	20	21	22	23	24	25		18	19	20	21	22	23	24
	26	27	28	29	30				25	26	27	28	29	30	31